Low Carb Counting

Gertrude Meckett

Copyright © [Year of First Publication] by [Author or Pen Name]

All rights reserved.

No portion of this book may be reproduced in any form without written permission from the publisher or author, except as permitted by U.S. copyright law.

Contents

INTRODUCTION 1

Chapter 1 2

Chapter 2 9

Chapter 3 29

INTRODUCTION

Crab meat is a popular and versatile type of seafood. It is also very healthy and a good addition to a balanced diet, as it contains many nutrients coupled with a low fat content.

Delightfully salty with a slight hint of mineral sweetness, crab delivers all the appeal of seafood without the fishy aftertaste that some people prefer to avoid. Available in varieties such as Dungeness and Alaskan King, this crustacean is caught and enjoyed all around the world.

Historians believe that crab was one of the earliest foods enjoyed by coastal populations. Archaeologists have uncovered the remains of crab and other edible marine animals along the Eritrean coast. Additional archaeological discoveries from the Chesapeake Bay area suggest that crab was also among the most popular foods for Native Americans and early colonists.

Today, crab is regarded as a plentiful source of easily caught meat in some areas and as a delicacy in others. China is the world's largest exporter of crab while the United States imports and consumes the most.

Chapter 1

WHAT ARE THE HEALTH BENEFITS OF CRAB?

Crab is an excellent addition to a healthy eating plan. It is low in calories with only around 85-90 per 100g (depending on crab type). It does contain some fat, but it is generally unsaturated fat which is considered heart healthy. Crab is also a natural source of omega-3 fatty acids, which can help to improve memory, decrease the chances of having a heart attack, decrease risk of cancer, and possibly help to improve depression and anxiety.

Crab is a low risk seafood for mercury. Many fish, particularly at the higher end of the food chain, contain dangerous amounts of mercury and are not recommended as frequently eaten foods. Crab contains many of the benefits of other seafood, but without the risk of mercury poisoning.

Crab is also a good source of vitamins A, C and the B vitamins including B12, and minerals like zinc and copper. It is a source of selenium, which may be a means of preventing cancer. Crab also has some chromium, which is considered a useful mineral if you have insulin resistance, as it may improve blood sugar metabolism.

CAUTIONS ABOUT CRAB

If you have an allergy to crab meat you should be careful not to eat it or dishes that may contain crab. If you are allergic to crab, you may also be allergic to other types of shellfish, including lobster and prawns. The symptoms of a crab allergy can be as minor as a skin rash or as dangerous as anaphylaxis, which can lead to death if not treated promptly. Crab also contains moderately large amounts of purines, which are necessary for the healthy functioning of the body, but in some individuals can cause gout.

Crab may also easily cause food poisoning if it is not treated and prepared correctly. Crab must be fresh, without a strong odor and should be kept cold or frozen if it is not eaten immediately.

Crab is an excellent addition to most diets, being low in fat and calories, but high in protien and nutrients. Crab can be prepared in many different ways which makes it easy to include in regular meals.

CRAB: ARE THERE HEALTH BENEFITS?

TOP 5 REASONS WHY EATING CRAB IS GOOD FOR YOU

It's widely known that the Food Standards Agency recommends eating 2 portions of fish per week – and living in Salcombe, this isn't too difficult.

However, we often get asked the question 'is crab good for you? and we're here to let you in on a little secret... crab may actually be more beneficial to human health than finfish!

The British shoreline is host to the pie crust edged brown crab (cancer Pagurus) which is caught and mostly shipped across the Channel to France and Spain. There it is consumed with gusto, mainly by us Brits abroad.

So why not enjoy crab when you are in the UK? Eating a portion of this nutritious crustacean has incredible health benefits when eaten regularly. Is crab good for you? The answer is a big juicy 'YES!'

1. CRAB IS A GREAT SOURCE OF PROTEIN

- Crab is one of the best possible dietary sources of protein available. Itcontains almost as much protein per 100 grammes as meats without anywhere near the same levels of saturated fat, which is linked to an increased risk of heart disease.

- The protein in crab is of high quality and, because of a lack ofconnective tissue, very digestible for people of all ages.

2. CRAB CONTAINS LONG-CHAIN OMEGA-3 FATTY ACIDS

- Rich in vitamins and minerals, crab meat is also low in fat and contains Omega-3 polyunsaturated acids.

- Helps provide protection from heart disease and aids brain development. Some research suggests that Omega-3 also inhibits aggressive behaviour.

- And it's not just any old Omega-3 – it's the long chain variety.

These are more beneficial to our health because they can be used immediately, unlike short-chain Omega-3 found in vegetables and oils; they need to be converted to the long chain form first which our bodies aren't very good at.

- 100g of crab provides a third of the UK recommended weekly intake of Omega-3.

3. CRAB CONTAINS SELENIUM

- All shellfish are a good source of Selenium but crab meat is particularly rich in it.

- Selenium plays a key role in the human's antioxidant defence system, preventing damage to cells and tissues.

- Selenium also plays an important role in the function of the immune system, in thyroid hormone metabolism and synthesis in reproduction.

- 100g of crab meat provides 112% of the daily recommended value for men and 140% daily recommended value for women. Crab meat contains 3 times the amount of Selenium than cod and 12 times that of beef!

4. CRAB CONTAINS RIBOFLAVIN (VITAMIN B2)

- As vitamins are water soluble, and therefore not stored in the body, they have to be obtained through our diet, such as through crab meat.

- Riboflavin (Vitamin B2) is important in the production of steroids and red blood cells, the promotion of normal growth, and the maintenance of the skin, eyes and the nervous system.

- Riboflavin also plays a role in iron absorption in the digestive tract andsupports the activity of antioxidants.

- And take note all you athletes and bodybuilders: turnover of Riboflavin in the human body is thought to be related to energy expenditure, and therefore physically active peoples may have an increased requirement of Riboflavin in their diet.

5. CRAB CONTAINS COPPER AND PHOSPHORUS

- Crab meat contains nearly 30 times the copper found in cod and 56 times that found in salmon, chicken and beef.

- Even though iron usually gets the spotlight, copper is involved in the absorption, storage and metabolism of iron. It is important in the formation of red blood cells and keeps bones, blood vessels, nerves and the immune system healthy.

- Phosphorus is after calcium the second most abundant mineral in the body. It is a principal mineral of bones and teeth and is, therefore, important in skeletal health and development.

- Phosphorus is involved in most metabolic actions in the body,including kidney functioning, cell growth and the contraction of the heart muscle. It is also involved in converting food to energy.

- 100g of crab provides 62% of daily recommended value for adult men and women.

HOW CARB COUNTING WORKS

Carb counting can help a person manage their risk of blood sugar spikes.

The first step in carb counting is identifying which foods contain carbohydrates and how rapidly these carbohydrates will boost blood sugar levels.

People can use a system called the Glycemic Index (GI) to calculate this. Every food has a GI ranking, with higher scores demonstrating a food's rapid effect on blood sugar.

Having diabetes often means that people struggle to regulate their blood sugar levels. So, it is also a good idea for people with diabetes to focus on their diet. Consuming low-GI foods can lead to a slower, more controllable increase in blood glucose levels.

Doctors and dietitians will help people with diabetes work out how many carbohydrates they should consume each day and suggest meal plans to help them maintain a healthful, nutritional balance.

Previously, doctors and dietitians suggested a typical range of carbohydrates that was a fit-all solution for everyone with diabetes.

Now, doctors and nutritionists work with individuals on a one-to-one basis to calculate the ideal daily caloric intake and carbohydrate percentages and servings each person needs.

These amounts will vary according to a range of factors, including the person's weight, height, activity levels, and whether they are taking medications.

Aims Of Carb Counting

Carb counting alone is not a substitute for managing diabetes using medical care and prescribed medications.

The goal of carb counting is to keep blood sugar levels steady for the following reasons:

- maintaining overall health in those with diabetes

- preventing the complications of excessively high or low blood sugar

- improving energy levels

GETTING STARTED WITH CARB COUNTING

Carb counting may help many people with diabetes to maintain steady blood sugar levels. However, it is only one way to manage diabetes.

Before trying carb counting, people should always speak with a nutritionist, diabetes educator, or doctor to determine:

- whether carb counting is appropriate

- the recommended daily allowance for carbohydrates

- which foods they recommend

Different people will require different amounts of carbohydrates depending on the type and severity of diabetes they have.

Speak to your doctor about the ideal calorie and carbohydrate intake.

Chapter 2

POSH CRAB PASTY

This coupled with glass of champagne - yes please!

Course Main Dish, Snack

Cuisine Italian

Prep Time 30 minutes

Cook Time 25 minutes

Passive Time 1 hour

Servings people

INGREDIENTS

- 1 knob butter
- 1 bunch spring onions chopped (including the green bits)
- 200 g white crabmeat
- 1 tbsp tarragon chopped
- 1 tbsp parsley chopped
- 0.5 each lemon zested
- 300 g all-butter shortcrust pastries
- 1 each free-range egg beaten

INSTRUCTIONS

1. Heat the oven to 200C/fan180C/gas 6. Melt a knob of butter in a pan. Cook the spring onions for a few minutes until softened. Cool then stir in the crab, tarragon, parsley, lemon zest and season.

2. Roll out the pastry to 20p thickness and then use side plates to cut out four circles, approx 16cm. Divide the crab mix between the circles, brush the edges with egg, then fold and crimp. Brush all over with egg. Bake for 20-25 minutes until golden. Serve warm or at room temperature

Nutrition Profile:

Low-Calorie Low Carbohydrate Nut-Free Soy-Free Healthy Pregnancy

Low Added Sugars

SPEEDY CRAB CAKES

Shallow-fry these easy crab cakes on the stovetop to get the perfect crisp crust without the greasy mess of deep-frying. Serve these cakes with CitrusArugula Salad (see associated recipe).

Active: 20 mins

Total: 20 mins

Servings: 4

Ingredients

- 1 large egg
- 2 tablespoons mayonnaise
- 2 teaspoons Dijon mustard
- ¼ teaspoon ground pepper
- Pinch of salt
- Pinch of cayenne pepper
- ¼ cup chopped scallions

- 12 ounces jumbo lump crabmeat, drained and picked over
- ¾ cup panko breadcrumbs, preferably whole-wheat
- 2 tablespoons extra-virgin olive oil
- Lemon wedges for serving

Directions

- **Step 1**

Whisk egg, mayonnaise, mustard, pepper, salt and cayenne in a medium bowl until combined. Stir in scallions. Add crab and panko; stir to combine. Form the mixture into four 1/2-inch-thick patties.

- **Step 2**

Heat oil in a large nonstick skillet over medium-high heat until shimmering. Add the crab cakes and cook, turning once, until golden brown, 4 to 5 minutes per side. Serve with lemon wedges.

Nutrition Facts Serving Size: 1 Crab Cake Per Serving:

265 calories; protein 22g; carbohydrates 11.2g; dietary fiber 1.7g; sugars 0.6g; fat 14.8g; saturated fat 2.2g; cholesterol 109.4mg; vitamin a iu 1 47.5IU; vitamin c 1.2mg; folate 10.3mcg; calcium 72.7mg; iron 1.2mg; magnesium 2.9mg; potassium 41.5mg; sodium 486.4mg.

Exchanges:

2 1/2 Fat, 2 1/2 Lean Protein, 1/2 Starch

Healthy Baked Crab Cakes Recipe

Total Time: 25 min

Prep Time: 10 min

Cook Time: 15 min

Servings: 4 (2 cakes each)

Crab cakes are so reminiscent of summer. Full of delicious crab, they can transport you to a coastal vacation without ever leaving your house.

By making them at home instead of ordering them from a restaurant or buying them pre-made at the store, you can control everything that goes into them. That means tons of fresh lump crab meat, just enough bread crumbs to hold them together, and fresh vegetables and spices for flavor. You can also control what stays out of them—lots of sodium and fat.

These healthy crab cakes are lightened up by baking instead of frying, using just a bit of whole wheat bread crumbs and no added salt. It's all served with a delicious spicy Greek yogurt dipping sauce.

Ingredients

- 1 egg plus 1 egg white
- 1 tablespoon dijon mustard
- Juice from 1 lemon
- 1/2 teaspoon paprika

- 1/4 teaspoon freshly cracked black pepper
- 8 ounces crab meat
- 1/2 cup whole wheat panko bread crumbs
- 2 cloves garlic, minced
- 1/2 jalapeno, minced
- 1 green onion, chopped
- Olive oil or oil spray
- 1/2 cup nonfat plain Greek yogurt
- 1 teaspoon dijon mustard
- 1 green onion, finely chopped
- Juice of 1/2 lemon
- 1/2 teaspoon cayenne
- Pinch freshly cracked black pepper

Preparation

1. Gather the ingredients.
2. Heat oven to 400F.
3. In a large bowl, whisk together eggs, dijon, lemon juice, paprika, and black pepper. Stir in crab, garlic, jalapeno, and green onion.

Gently stir in bread crumbs until just combined.

4. Form mixture into 8 patties and place on a baking sheet lined with parchment or a silicone baking mat. Lightly brush or spray the tops of each with olive oil.

5. Bake for 15 minutes or until the tops are lightly golden. Remove from the oven and serve with sauce.

6. To make the sauce, whisk together all ingredients from Greek yogurt through cracked black pepper, until smooth.

Ingredient Variations and Substitutions

Add more or less jalapeno and cayenne pepper based on your preferred spice level.

Cooking and Serving Tips

Make it easy on yourself by buying crab meat that has already been shelled. It should be near the seafood counter at the grocery store.

If you can't find whole wheat bread crumbs, make your own! Toast a slice of whole wheat bread until crispy, then blend in the food processor until large crumbs form.

Try these cakes over a green salad for lunch or share them with friends as a delicious summer appetizer.

LOW CARB CRAB SALAD RECIPE – PALEO FRIENDLY

This tasty low carb cold salad with crab meat has the usual spices but adds a hint of sweetener. Stevia is used to enhance the flavor without adding unnecessary carbs. **Prep Time5** mins

Total Time 5 mins

Servings 4 people

Calories 164

Ingredients

12 ounces crab meat fresh or canned

1 cup chopped celery

¼ cup avocado mayonnaise

1 teaspoon celery seed

1 low carb sugar substitute packet(s)

¼ teaspoon ground black pepper

½ teaspoon Old Bay Seasoning TM

1 teaspoons dried parsley

Instructions

1. In a large bowl, combine the crabmeat, celery, mayonnaise, celery seed, stevia, pepper, seafood seasoning and parsley until well mixed.

2. Refrigerate until chilled.

Nutrition Fact

Serving: 0.5cup | Calories: 164 | Carbohydrates: 1g | Protein: 17g | Fat: 10g |

Saturated Fat: 2g | Polyunsaturated Fat: 6g | Monounsaturated Fat: 3g |

Cholesterol: 103mg | Sodium: 522mg | Potassium: 78mg | Fiber: 1g |

Vitamin A: 100IU | Vitamin C: 1.7mg | Calcium: 110mg | Iron: 4.3mg

Additional Info

Net Carbs: 0 g | % Carbs: 0 % | % Protein: 43 % | % Fat: 57 % |

SmartPoints: 4

Note on Nutritional Information

Nutritional information for the recipe is provided as a courtesy and is approximate only. We cannot guarantee the accuracy of the nutritional information given for any recipe on this site. Erythritol carbs are not included in carb counts as it has been shown not to impact blood sugar. Net carbs are the total carbs minus fiber.

Low-Carb Crab Cakes (Keto)

Ditch the bread crumbs and try these low-carb crab cakes instead! You still get the perfect golden exterior and wonderful crab flavor without all the unwanted carbs or gluten. **Prep Time**:5 minutes

Cook Time:10 minutes

Chill Time:15 minutes **Total Time**:30 minutes **Servings**:

Ingredients

8 ounces lump, canned, or fresh crab meat

2 small shallots (diced)

¼cup green pepper (diced)

2 tablespoons green onions (chopped)

½cupalmond flour

1. large egg

2. tablespoons mayonnaise

2 teaspoons Old Bay seasoning

1. tablespoon Worcestershiresauce

¼ teaspoon pepper

½ teaspoon salt

1. tablespoonsolive oil (for frying)

Parsley (chopped — for serving)

Instructions

1. In a large mixing bowl, add all of the ingredients for the crab cakes.

2. Mix the ingredients until well-combined.

3. Form the mixture into 4 small patties and chill in the refrigerator for 15 minutes.

4. In a large frying pan over medium-high heat, add the olive oil.

5. Once the oil is hot, add the patties and fry for about 5 minutes per side until they are cooked through and golden brown on each side.

Recipe Notes

This recipe is for 2 servings. Each serving includes 2 crab cakes.

I recommend serving with chopped parsley and tartar sauce.

Leftover crab cakes can be stored in an airtight container in the refrigerator for up to 3 days.

Nutrition Info Per Serving

Nutrition Facts

Low-Carb Crab Cakes

Amount Per Serving (2 crab cakes)

Calories 388Calories from Fat 244 % Daily Value* Fat 27.1g42% Saturated

Fat 4.1g21% Trans Fat 0g Polyunsaturated Fat 7.7g Monounsaturated Fat 10.6g Cholesterol 264mg88% Sodium1806.7mg75% Potassium 193.3mg6% Carbohydrates 7.4g2% Fiber 2.7g11% Sugar 3.2g4% Protein 31.1g62% Net carbs 4.7g* Percent Daily Values are based on a 2000 calorie diet.

SKINNY SHRIMP AND CRAB SALAD

Skinny Shrimp and Crab Salad is good by itself, served on a bed of lettuce, with crackers, or as a sandwich! Serves 4 entree size salads on top of 2 cups of lettuce. Makes 6 sandwiches or pitas.

Prep Time10 mins

Cook Time1 min

Total Time10 mins

Ingredients

- 6 ounces 100-150 count shrimp, cooked
- 12 ounces crab meat flaked
- ½ to ¾ cup olive oil mayonnaise
- 1 Tablespoon green onions diced
- 1 Tablespoon Ranch dressing mix

- ⅛ teaspoon freshly ground black pepper
- ⅛ teaspoon creole seasoning
- ⅛ teaspoon salt
- 1 teaspoon McCormick Salad Supreme

Instructions

1. Drain shrimp and crab and pat dry with a paper towel.
2. In a large bowl, combine all ingredients except shrimp and crab; stir until combined.
3. Add shrimp and crab and stir carefully so as to not break up crab.
4. Refrigerate at least 30 minutes before serving.

Nutrition Fact

Calories: 192kcal | Carbohydrates: 5g | Protein: 24g | Fat: 7g | Saturated Fat:

1g | Cholesterol: 147mg | Sodium: 1604mg | Potassium: 208mg | Sugar: 1g |

Vitamin A: 81IU | Vitamin C: 8mg | Calcium: 101mg | Iron: 1mg

Crab Shack Summer Salad

This grilled corn and crab salad is healthy, quick and easy to make, and perfect for a cool dinner on a hot summer night. PREP TIME 20 mins

COURSE Main Course, Salad

SERVINGS 4 Dinner Size Servings

CALORIES 263 kcal

INGREDIENTS

- 3 ears of corn grilled and cooled
- 1 cup cherry or grape tomatoes sliced in half
- 1-14 ounce can hearts of palm drained and sliced 1/2-inch thick
- 1 cup jumbo lump crab meat rinsed and any shell pieces removed
- 1 Hass avocado pitted and cut into 1-inch pieces
- 1/4 cup very thinly sliced sweet onion
- 1/4 cup coarsely chopped herbs - parsley basil and chives

Dressing

- 1/4 cup plain nonfat Greek yogurt

- 2 tablespoons olive oil

- juice and zest of 1 lime

- 1/8 teaspoon curry powder

- salt and pepper to taste

INSTRUCTIONS

1. Slice the corn from the cob, and place in a large mixing bowl.

2. Add tomatoes, heart of palm slices, crab meat, avocado pieces, onionsand parsley to the corn, and toss to combine.

3. In a separate bowl or measuring cup, combine ingredients for dressing and whisk well.

4. Pour dressing over salad and toss gently to combine.

5. Serve immediately.

RECIPIES NOTES

Recipe adapted from Food and Wine

NUTRITION FACT

Calories: 263kcalCarbohydrates: 21gProtein: 12gFat: 15gSaturated Fat:

2gCholesterol: 18mgSodium: 377mgPotassium: 773mgFiber: 5gSugar: 7gVitamin A: 700IUVitamin C: 27.3mgCalcium: 48mgIron: 1.5mg

Keto Crab Stuffed Avocado

Ingredients (makes 2 servings)

- 1/4 cup mayonnaise, store-bought or homemade, p. 112 in the cookbook (55 g/ 1.9 oz)
- 3 tbsp + 1 tsp lime juice, divided
- 2 tbsp diced onion (20 g/ 0.7 oz)
- 2 tbsp chopped fresh cilantro
- 1/2 tsp ground cumin
- 1/4 tsp fine sea salt
- pinch of fresh ground pepper

- 1 can crabmeat (170 g/ 6 oz)

- 1 ripe Haas avocado, halved, pitted and peeled (200 g/ 7.1 oz)

- lime wedges, for serving

- **Optional**: Green Goddess Dressing, for drizzling (p. 117 in the cookbook)

Instructions

1. In a medium bowl, combine the mayonnaise, 3 tablespoons of the lime juice, onions, cilantro, cumin, salt, and pepper. Gently fold in the crabmeat. Taste for seasoning and add more salt and pepper if desired.

Brush the avocado halves with the remaining 1 teaspoon of the lime juice to prevent discolouration.

Place the avocado halves, cut side up, on plates. Mound the crab salad into each avocado half. Serve with lime wedges and drizzle with Green Goddess Dressing, if desired.

Crab-Salad Cups Recipe

- **Total Time** 17m

- **Prep Time** 7 m

- **Calories** 181

Crab Louie salad or crab salad is also known as the "King of Salads." Hailing from Westcoast region of America, Crab-Salad has paved its way to the global cuisine with its exotic and outstanding taste. Salads have been the primary side dishes for many ages and have also been known for their low calorie count. If you are a seafood lover, then you would agree to the fact that there isn't anything more delightful than a crab. However, if your are health conscious and want to relish crabs in a healthy way, then here's a simple recipe that you can prepare in just 15 minutes. The traditional way of serving this dish is eye-grabbing, so even when you make it at home don't forget to amp up the way you serve it! Crabs can be quite filling, so this Crab-Salad can make for a wholesome meal. Drizzle some lemon juice to give this salad a fresh touch and garnish with cilantro. So follow us through this recipe and woo your loved ones!

Ingredients of Crab-Salad Cups

- 250 gm crab meat

- 1/2 cup mayonnaise

- 6 drops lemon juice

- 1 teaspoon mustard paste

- 3 tablespoon sour cream

- 2 celery

- 2 tablespoon tarragon

For Garnishing

- 3 sprigs cilantro

How to make Crab-Salad Cups

- **Step 1 Clean and boil the crab meat**

To make this amazing salad, begin with cleaning the crab meat with lukewarm water and then drain the excess water. Next, take a deep bottomed pan and boil crab meat for around 10 minutes and transfer it to a bowl.

- **Step 2 Add all the other ingredients and mix**

In the same bowl, add chopped celery, chives and tarragon, mayonnaise, sour cream, mustard and lemon juice and mix well.

- **Step 3 Serve it the way you like!**

You can make cups out of anything you prefer, we have used grapefruit cover as a cup to serve this amazing salad. Garnish with some cilantro and indulge in the goodness.

Chapter 3

CALCULATING CARBS

When a person has to calculate how many carbs they can consume each day, it is vital to know which foods contain carbohydrates, how many they contain, and their caloric and GI value.

In general, 1 gram (g) of carbohydrate provides around 4 calories. This can help a person calculate how many calories a particular snack or meal is providing.

There is no single number of carbs that is safe for every person with diabetes. Doctors shape the target based on individual needs and disease progression.

It is essential for those with diabetes to understand the content of food nutrition labels. Some describe nutrient serving per half portion, so it is necessary to be sure of exactly how many carbs a meal provides.

When reading nutritional labels, take note of the total number of carbohydrates per serving and add these totals into the total daily carbohydrate allowance.

For example, there are approximately 15 g of carbohydrate in each serving of the following foods:

- a slice of bread

- one-third of a cup of pasta or rice

- a small apple

- one tablespoon of jelly

- a half-cup of starchy vegetables, such as mashed potatoes.

However, non-starchy vegetables contain only 5 g of carbohydrate per serving. This means that a person with diabetes can safely eat three times more non-starchy vegetables than starchy vegetables.

CARB COUNTING TIPS

Carb counting may be challenging at first because it forces people to think about meals differently, and people might take a while to get used to it.

Some tips can help make carb counting a little easier, such as:

- **Counting mixed foods by the cup:** On average, a fist is the size of a 1-cup serving. For a mixed dish, this is an effective way to judge the carb totals based on cup size.

- **Count tablespoons:** It is helpful to know the number of carbohydrates in a tablespoon of food. People can count level tablespoons to create a healthful plate.

- **Count carbs in pizza using the crust:** If possible, choose a thin-crust pizza. This will save 5–10 g of carbohydrate per serving size when compared to a slice of regular or pan pizza.

- **Smoothies may not always be the best bet:** On average, a 12ounce (oz.) smoothie might contain more carbohydrates than a regular soda if it contains juice. Drink smoothies in moderation.

-

CRAB AND LEEK TART

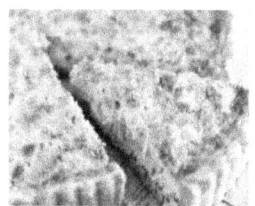

Crab is the quintessential taste of the British shoreline and partners perfectly with leek in this tempting tart recipe. The rich brown meat is really important in this crab recipe in order to give the tart a crabby oomph of flavour!

Crab and Leek Tart

This must be the best crab and leek tart I have ever seen. I could eat this every single day.

Course Main Dish

Cuisine British

Prep Time 10 minutes

Cook Time 20 minutes

Passive Time 1 hour

Servings people

INGREDIENTS

For the Pastry

- 100 g plain flour, plus extra for rolling
- 100 g wholemeal flour
- 125 g cold butter cubed

For the Filling

- 1 knob butter
- 50 each leeks trimmed, sliced thinly
- 50 g butter
- 300 ml crème fraîche half-fat
- 3 each free-range eggs beaten
- 100 g brown crab meat from Salcombe
- 1 pinch sea salt flakes
- 100 g white crab meat
- 50 g mature cheddar finely grated

- 1 each freshly ground black pepper

INSTRUCTIONS

For the pastry

1. Preheat the oven to 200C/400F/Gas 6

2. Pulse the flours and butter in a food processor until the mixture resembles fine breadcrumbs. With the motor running, add the egg in a thin stream and blend until the mixture begins to form a ball.

3. Roll the pastry into a circle on a floured work surface and use it to line a 23cm/9in loose-based fluted tart tin. Press the pastry with your fingertips firmly into the base and sides. Trim any excess pastry and lightly prick the base of the tart using a fork. Chill in the fridge for 30 minutes.

4. Line the pastry with a large sheet of crumpled baking parchment and half fill with baking beans. Bake the tart case for 25 minutes. Remove the beans and return the tart to the oven for a further 5-10 minutes or until the surface is dry and beginning to brown. Remove from the oven and reduce the oven to 160C/300F/Gas 4. ***For the filling***

5. Melt the butter in a large heavy-based frying pan over a low heat. Add the leeks and fry gently for 2-3 minutes, stirring until just softened.

Remove from the heat and set aside.

1. Put the eggs in a large jug and beat lightly with a whisk. Stir

in the crème fraîche, season with salt and freshly ground black pepper. Beat together with a wooden spoon until thoroughly combined. Stir in the brown crab meat.

2. Scatter the leeks over the pastry case and dot the white crab meat around them. Pour over the crème Fraiche mixture and sprinkle with the cheese. Cook on the baking tray for 25 minutes, or until the filling is golden brown and just set. (It should still wobble a tiny bit in the centre as it will continue to set as it cools.)

3. Remove the tart from the oven and leave to cool in the tin for 15 minutes before removing

CRAB AND PEA RISOTTO WITH BASIL

It's mid May and the waters around South Devon have warmed up slightly after the cold winter. This is a simple, Springtime meal to satisfy those taste buds now that crab is back in season.

The warmer waters mean that Salcombe crabs are venturing out from their mini hibernation in the mud and from under rocks to satisfy their appetites and build themselves up to full strength. As the crabs eat more food, each crab will yield greater amounts of meat as we build up towards a crescendo in Autumn. Time to get going with some creative crab recipes such as this one below. If you feel like adding some richness to the recipe, add some brown crab meat for a real punch of flavour.

Crab and Pea Risotto with Basil

Tasty crab and pea risotto recipe that you will just simply love!

Course Main Dish

Cuisine British

Prep Time 20 minutes

Cook Time 20 minutes

Passive Time 1 hour

Servings people

INGREDIENTS

- 1 knob butter
- 1 splash olive oil
- 1 each small onion finely chopped
- 150 g risotto rice arborio
- 1 clove garlic crushed
- 0.5 each red chilli finely chopped, or a pinch dried chilli flakes
- 700 ml vegetable stock at a simmer
- 75 g petits pois
- 2 tbsp mascarpone (optional)
- 1 each lemon zested and cut into wedges
- 100 g white crab meat

- 1 handful basil

INSTRUCTIONS

1. Heat a small knob of butter and 1 tbsp olive oil in a wide, shallow pan and fry the onion for 5 minutes. Add the rice, garlic and chilli, stir for 2 minutes, then splash in the wine and let it bubble away.

2. Pour in a third of the stock then simmer, stirring occasionally, until it is absorbed into the rice. Repeat twice until the rice is tender and creamy - about 15-20 minutes in all.

3. Tip in the peas for the final minute or two, then take the pan off the heat and swirl in the mascarpone, lemon zest and a squeeze of juice. Cover the pan and leave for 5 minutes. To serve, fold in the crabmeat and some torn basil leaves, then season. Serve with more basil and lemon wedges.

CRAB LINGUINE WITH CHILLI AND PARSLEY

As every crab lover knows, the brown meat packs a far bigger punch of flavour than the white. What we love best about this crab recipe is that it uses the wonderfully rich brown crab meat as a highly flavoured sauce to coat the linguine.

Crab Linguine with Chilli and Parsley

This coupled with a hint of chilli is absolutely divine. And it is the hen crab (the female) that produces much more of the brown meat than the cock crab (the male).

Course Main Dish

Cuisine Italian

Prep Time 20 minutes

Cook Time 30 minutes

Passive Time 1 hour

Servings people

INGREDIENTS

- 400 g linguine
- 4 tbsp extra-virgin olive oil
- 1 each red chilli deseeded and chopped
- 150 g risotto rice arborio
- 2 clove garlic crushed
- 200 g white crab meat
- 100 g brown crab meat
- 5 tbsp white wine

- 1 squeeze lemon (optional)

- 1 handful flat-leaf parsley leaves very finely chopped

INSTRUCTIONS

1. Bring a large pan of salted water to the boil and add the linguine. Give it a good stir and boil for 1 min less than the pack says. Stir well occasionally so it doesn't stick.

2. While the pasta cooks, gently heat 3 tbsp of olive oil with the chilli and garlic in a pan large enough to hold all the pasta comfortably. Cook the chilli and garlic very gently until they start to sizzle, then turn up the heat and add the white wine. Simmer everything until the wine and olive oil come together. Then take off the heat and add the brown crab meat, using a wooden spatula or spoon to mash it into the olive oil to make a thick sauce.

3. When the pasta has had its cooking time, taste a strand - it should have a very slight bite. When it's ready, turn off the heat. Place the sauce on a very low heat and use a pair of kitchen tongs to lift the pasta from the water into the sauce.

4. Off the heat, add the white crab meat and parsley to the pasta with a sprinkling of sea salt. Stir everything together really well, adding a drop of pasta water if it's starting to get claggy. Taste for seasoning

and, if it needs a slight lift, add a small squeeze of lemon. Serve immediately twirled into pasta bowls and drizzled with the remaining oil.

www.ingramcontent.com/pod-product-compliance
Lightning Source LLC
Chambersburg PA
CBHW072138070526
44585CB00016B/1730